THIS BOOK BELONGS TO

For my family and friends.

This book is dedicated to those fighting for wild forests,
clean mountains, and a safe climate future.

J.M.

With highest gratitude to Dr Linden Ashcroft, Dr Hazel Richards,
Dr. Tom Fairman, Dr. Karen Rowe, Caroline Foster, and Alice Sutherland-Hawes
for their time and expert knowledge.

HIGH

JESS McGEACHIN

WELBECK
EDITIONS

Published in 2023 by Welbeck Editions
An Imprint of Welbeck Children's Limited, part of Welbeck Publishing Group.
20 Mortimer Street London W1T 3JW

Text and illustrations © Jess McGeachin 2023

Jess McGeachin has asserted his moral right to be identified as the author and Illustrator
of this Work in accordance with the Copyright Designs and Patents Act 1988.

Associate Publishers: Laura Knowles and Gemma Farr
Design: Sam James and Jess McGeachin

FSC
www.fsc.org
MIX
Paper | Supporting
responsible forestry
FSC® C020056

A CIP catalogue record for this book is available from
the Library of Congress

978-1-80338-046-9

Printed in Heshan, China

10 9 8 7 6 5 4 3 2 1

CONTENTS

PREPARE FOR TAKE OFF

Buckle your seatbelt, stretch out your wings and get ready to take to the skies. We're on a journey to the highest places on Earth, from the tallest trees to soaring skyscrapers and the mountain peaks that overshadow them all.

This is the world of the climbers and the fliers. Sharp claws and warm fur will come in handy, and a few extra feathers will help too. Pack oxygen—the air up here can get pretty thin.

You can borrow a ride of course; take your pick from wooden gliders, buoyant balloons, or a golden chariot of the gods.

As your feet leave the ground, Earth gets smaller and smaller below. High places have a way of putting things into perspective and our home looks very fragile from up here.

All set? Three, two, one... lift off!

BIRD'S EYE VIEW

If you're going to spend a lot of time high above, good eyesight is a must. Raptors like hawks and eagles have large forward-facing eyes which give them excellent depth perception—handy for spying dinner far below.

LEAFY GREEN

Leaves are like mini solar panels, converting sunlight into energy. They use a chemical called chlorophyll, which to our eyes looks green. As the seasons change and there's less light, the level of chlorophyll drops—turning deciduous leaves from lush green into reds and yellows.

TREES THAT TALK

The forest has a lot to say if you have the time to listen. Songbirds whistle to mark their territory. Squirrels scurry to find a winter hoard. Even the trees whisper to each other through chemicals in the air or their secret fungal network.

HIGH LIFE

We spend a lot of our lives looking out in front or down at our feet, but not much time looking up. Here, between the knotted tree crowns and the leafy canopy, sits a whole new world. Swooping and gliding are the movements of choice up above, and if you build the right home you might never need to come down.

SAFE ABOVE

The high life has its advantages. It's cool and shady in the summer, there's plenty to eat, and it's a long way from predators below. It's a great place to make a nest, but don't forget there could be dangers circling even higher above.

ANCIENT GIANTS

If you've ever been told to stand still like a tree, you can actually dance around as much as you like. Trees don't stay still—they are constantly on the move, inching upwards to get more sunlight or sprawling outwards to find better balance.

Some, like the giant sequoias, can live for thousands of years. Imagine what they've seen in their lifetime or what they will see when we're gone.

Yellow meranti
Up to 300ft high

HERE COMES THE SUN

Like most plants, trees make energy using the sun. But what if your neighbour is getting in the way of your sweet rays? You'll have to grow taller than they do. With the right combination of water and nutrients trees can grow to extraordinary heights.

Baobab tree
Up to 100ft high

Kapok tree
Up to 200ft high

BACK TO YOUR ROOTS

Many tall trees grow deep roots, but if the soil is too shallow they might need a buttress. These giant above-ground roots help stabilise the tree, just like training wheels on a bike. Giant redwoods grow close to each other so their roots can cling together and give them a bit of extra support.

GROWING UP SUCKS

Trees suck in water through their roots and up their trunk. It's a lot of work, and the taller the tree the harder it gets. But redwoods have got a neat party trick—because they live in a foggy climate, they're able to absorb water directly through their leaves and save all that energy for growing.

Coastal redwood
Up to 380ft high

Giant sequoia
Up to 280ft high

Karri tree
Up to 280ft high

Mountain ash
Up to 330ft high

NICE RING TO IT

Trees have long memories. Dendrochronologists are scientists who study tree time. They can read the rings of a tree trunk to learn what was happening hundreds of years ago. A wider ring was a warm, wet year while a thinner one was cold and dry.

TREE DWELLERS

Arboreal animals are creatures who spend most (or all) of their time in trees. They've adapted to canopy life in lots of different ways—growing sharp claws, talented tails and even stretchy skin so they never have to touch the ground.

Koala

Tree kangaroo

SLOW AND STEADY

The leaf diet doesn't hold a lot of nutritional value. Salad-loving animals like koalas and sloths need to eat a lot and take life at a pretty slow pace to conserve energy (if they're not already asleep that is).

THE WAY YOU MOVE

Life is all about balance. Many arboreal animals have a low centre of gravity to stop themselves falling off narrow branches. A tail is helpful for balance too, or you could try sticky slime like a tree snail.

Binturong

Chameleon

Tree snail

Green tree python

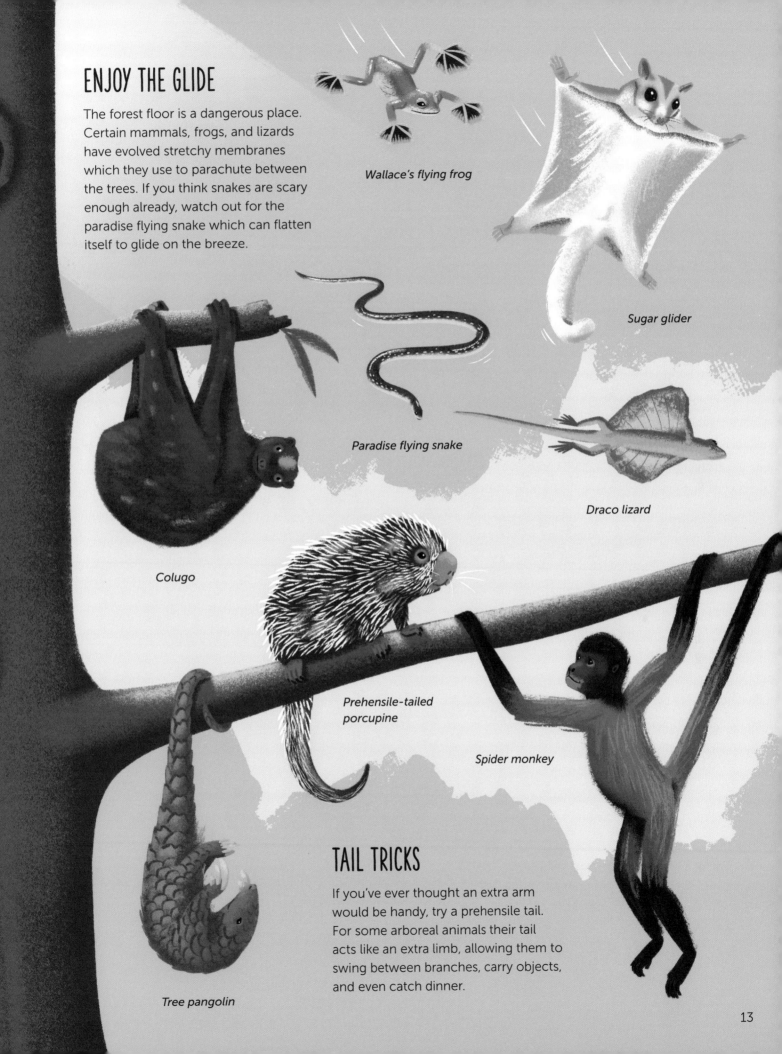

ENJOY THE GLIDE

The forest floor is a dangerous place. Certain mammals, frogs, and lizards have evolved stretchy membranes which they use to parachute between the trees. If you think snakes are scary enough already, watch out for the paradise flying snake which can flatten itself to glide on the breeze.

Wallace's flying frog

Sugar glider

Paradise flying snake

Draco lizard

Colugo

Prehensile-tailed porcupine

Spider monkey

TAIL TRICKS

If you've ever thought an extra arm would be handy, try a prehensile tail. For some arboreal animals their tail acts like an extra limb, allowing them to swing between branches, carry objects, and even catch dinner.

Tree pangolin

13

NESTS AND NOOKS

All creatures want to keep their kids safe, so a home out of harm's way is a must. Those who are handy with their beaks might weave a cozy nest. Others might find a ready-made hollow—or simply steal someone else's place.

African weaver nest

Hummingbird nest

Robin nest

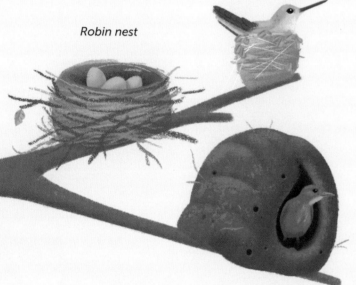

Baya weaver nest

Red ovenbird nest

WONDERFUL WEAVERS

Nature has some nifty knitters. Weaver birds stitch grass and twigs together, hummingbirds sew with stolen spiderwebs and the red ovenbird makes its dome-shaped nest with mud, clay, and a little bit of poop.

Montezuma oropendola nest

ROOM FOR ONE MORE?

Sociable weavers like apartment living. Over generations these African songbirds build huge hanging homes where dozens of families can live. The nests stay cool in the desert heat, warm at night, and are even rented out to other bird species.

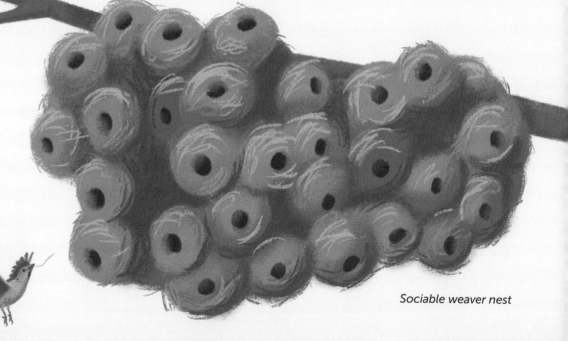

Sociable weaver nest

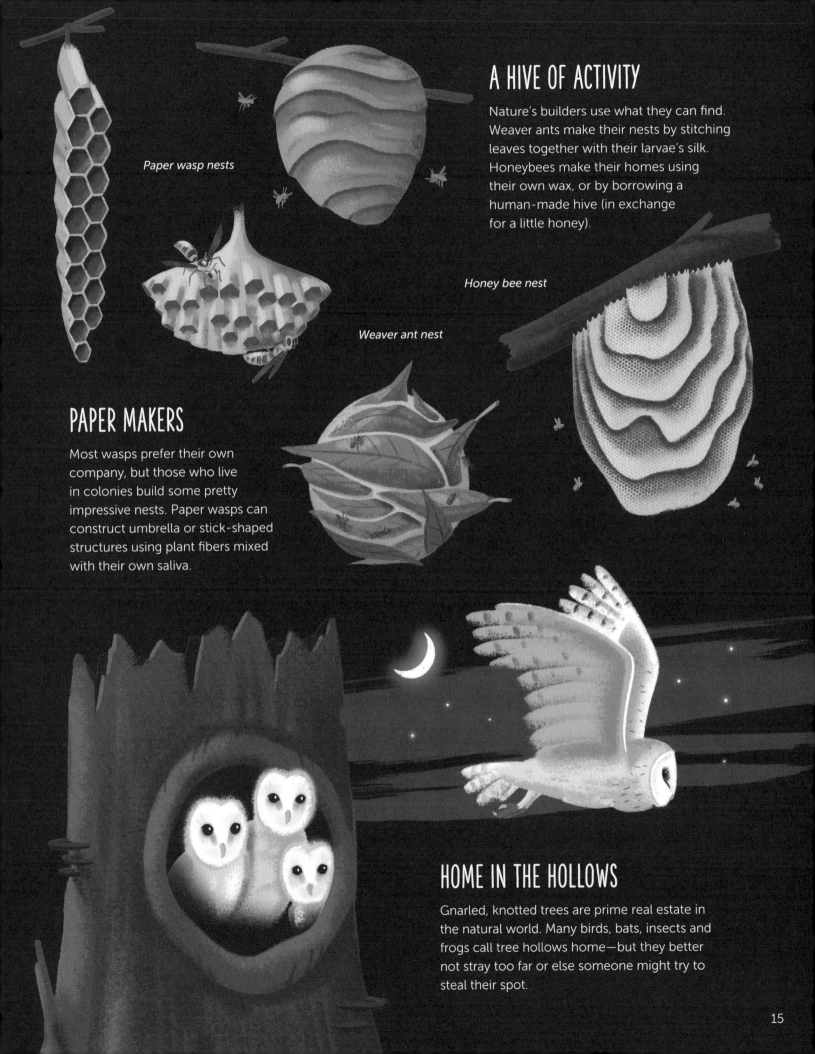

A HIVE OF ACTIVITY

Nature's builders use what they can find. Weaver ants make their nests by stitching leaves together with their larvae's silk. Honeybees make their homes using their own wax, or by borrowing a human-made hive (in exchange for a little honey).

Paper wasp nests

Honey bee nest

Weaver ant nest

PAPER MAKERS

Most wasps prefer their own company, but those who live in colonies build some pretty impressive nests. Paper wasps can construct umbrella or stick-shaped structures using plant fibers mixed with their own saliva.

HOME IN THE HOLLOWS

Gnarled, knotted trees are prime real estate in the natural world. Many birds, bats, insects and frogs call tree hollows home—but they better not stray too far or else someone might try to steal their spot.

FADING FORESTS

Look at the land from high above and you'll see a patchwork painting in yellow and green. Except the colours are changing, and places that were once dense rainforests are now flattened farmland. We're losing our forests at a faster pace than ever before, but it's not too late to repaint the picture.

FIND ME IN THE FOREST

From temperate woodlands to lush jungles and frosted snow taiga, more than half of the land animals on Earth call the forest home. But it's a home under threat—humans have cleared a third of all forests on the planet in the last hundred years, and we haven't slowed down yet.

OLDER AND WISER

Old-growth forests are messy places. Full of ancient trees, knotted hollows, and a damp layer of decay, they store a huge amount of carbon and are home to many threatened species. But we're not letting them grow old, and now more than ever we need to share in their secrets.

REWILDING

Nature has an extraordinary ability to heal herself. Sometimes people can help through restoring native forests or reintroducing key species, but the best place to start is by protecting the wild places we have left right now. They might even keep us safe in return.

LIFE IN THE CLOUDS

More than half of us live in urban areas like cities. They can be exciting places, bustling with things to do and places to be. A skyscraper might be used as a place to work or as a home to thousands of people under the same roof.

SKY'S THE LIMIT

In Greek mythology, it was never a good idea to get too close to the sun. Modern skyscrapers are soaring to extraordinary heights but sometimes it's easy to lose perspective of the changes happening down below.

HIGH RISE

As you walk around a big city
you might start to get a sore neck.
Up here the world is mirrored in glass,
and it's getting taller all of the time.
People build high for lots of different
reasons—to honor their gods, to
remember their kings and queens,
or to keep watch over their enemies.
It's a nice view, but then again the birds
have always known that.

NESTS WITH A VIEW

Tall cities aren't just for people.
Peregrine falcons have been
known to nest high on the side of
skyscrapers, watching the workers
far below. Pigeons like city life
too—who said there was no such
thing as a free lunch?

TOMBS AND TEMPLES

What happens when we die? Is there someone up above we should be keeping happy? Where does belly button fluff come from?

These are questions we've been asking since ancient times. It was thought that building monumental structures might help find the answers, and we've been building steadily higher ever since.

Stonehenge
2500 BCE

Unstan Chambered Cairn
3400 BCE

SET IN STONE

Some of the very first human-made structures were stacks of balanced stone called cairns. They were used as burial sites for important people, places of worship or maybe even to map the stars across the night sky.

MADE TO LAST

The great pyramid of Giza was built as a tomb for the pharaoh Khufu. It was the tallest human-made structure on earth for nearly 4,000 years, but its surface wasn't always dusty stone—it was once covered in a smooth, white limestone gleaming in the desert sun.

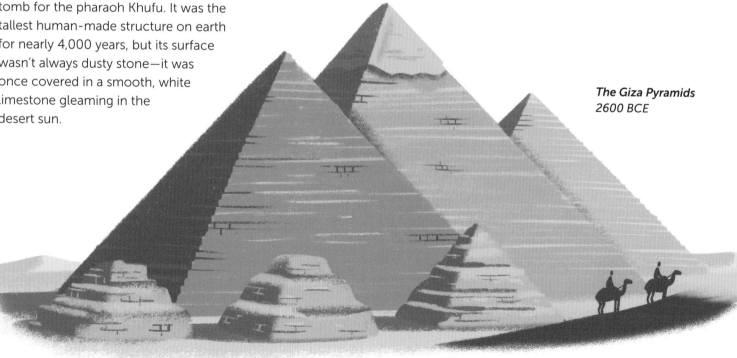

The Giza Pyramids
2600 BCE

Great Stupa
300 BCE

Ruiguang Pagoda
247 CE

Brahmeswara Temple
1058 CE

Great Mosque of Samarra
848 CE

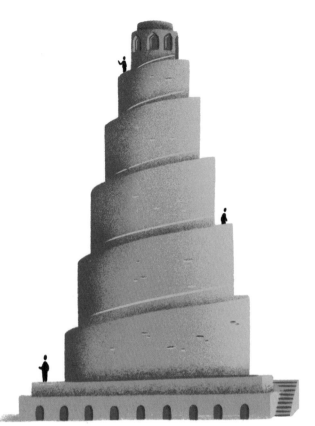

Chartres Cathedral
1145 CE

BUILT TO IMPRESS

As building techniques advanced, so too did the ambition of the people building them. Ancient cultures constructed spiral temples, wooden pagodas and complex cathedrals, all with the goal of standing out from a distance—which many of them still do today.

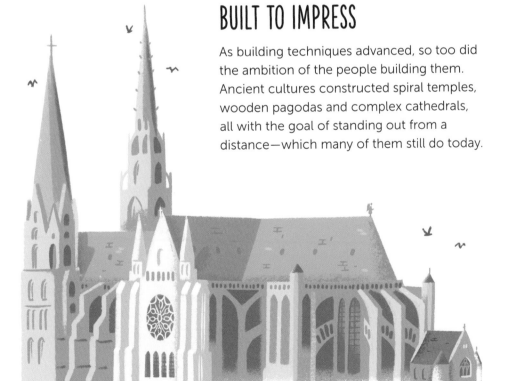

LEAVE NO TRACE

We tend to celebrate cultures that leave big things behind. Walls, pyramids, monuments to men on horses. But with all the scars we've created on our planet, maybe we should look to those who have left songs and stories to share instead.

KEEPING WATCH

In dynasties past, keeping an eye on your enemies meant building high walls and watchtowers.

The Great Wall of China snakes across arid deserts to soaring mountain peaks. This monumental structure was used to move soldiers and supplies across vast distances and guard against invaders from the north.

GOOD ENOUGH TO EAT

It's always a good idea to play with your food. Much of the Great Wall is held together with sticky rice mortar—a combination of slaked lime and sweet rice flour. It's surprisingly strong when set and has helped the wall withstand armies and earthquakes for centuries. Not recommended for lunch.

ALONG THE WATCHTOWER

For urgent messages along the Great Wall, the post probably wasn't quick enough. When an intruder was spotted, soldiers would create smoke signals by day, or light blazing beacons at night. There was even a code to show how great the threat was— one fire and a cannon shot meant "send a hundred men" while many fires meant "wake up everyone you can find."

BACK TO NATURE

The natural world doesn't seem to take much notice of borders. High in the mountains, parts of the wall are starting to crumble. Golden eagles cross high above while trees slowly grow where soldiers once stood—maybe it's us they're keeping watch for.

EVER HIGHER

A hundred years ago, buildings that soared over 1,000 feet were ground-breaking skyscrapers. In our century that height has more than doubled, with the Burj Khalifa piercing the clouds 2,717 feet in the sky.

These monoliths take a huge amount of energy to build, and it might be time to ask how high is high enough?

RACE TO THE TOP

Competition makes people do strange things. In the 1930s, the designers of the Chrysler, 40 Wall Street and Empire State Building were locked in a fight for height, each adding more floors to their building to become the tallest. The Empire State won, and remained the tallest building in the world for nearly forty years.

THE RISE OF STEEL

There's only so high you can build with stone or brick, and the taller you go the thicker the walls need to be. The use of steel beams in the late nineteenth century changed all of that, allowing engineers to build spanning skyscrapers that still shape the skyline today.

FIND YOUR FOOTING

Skyscrapers are designed to sway with the wind, anchored by deep foundations in the bedrock. And if the ground is made up of sand and shells? Try wearing giant, concrete flip-flops like the Burj Khalifa and let friction do the rest.

Burj Khalifa
2,717ft high

Jeddah Tower
(Under Construction)
3,300+ft high

Taipei 101
1,667ft high

Petronas Towers
1,483ft high

Empire State Building
1,453ft high

Chrysler Building
1,046ft high

Eiffel Tower
1,060ft high

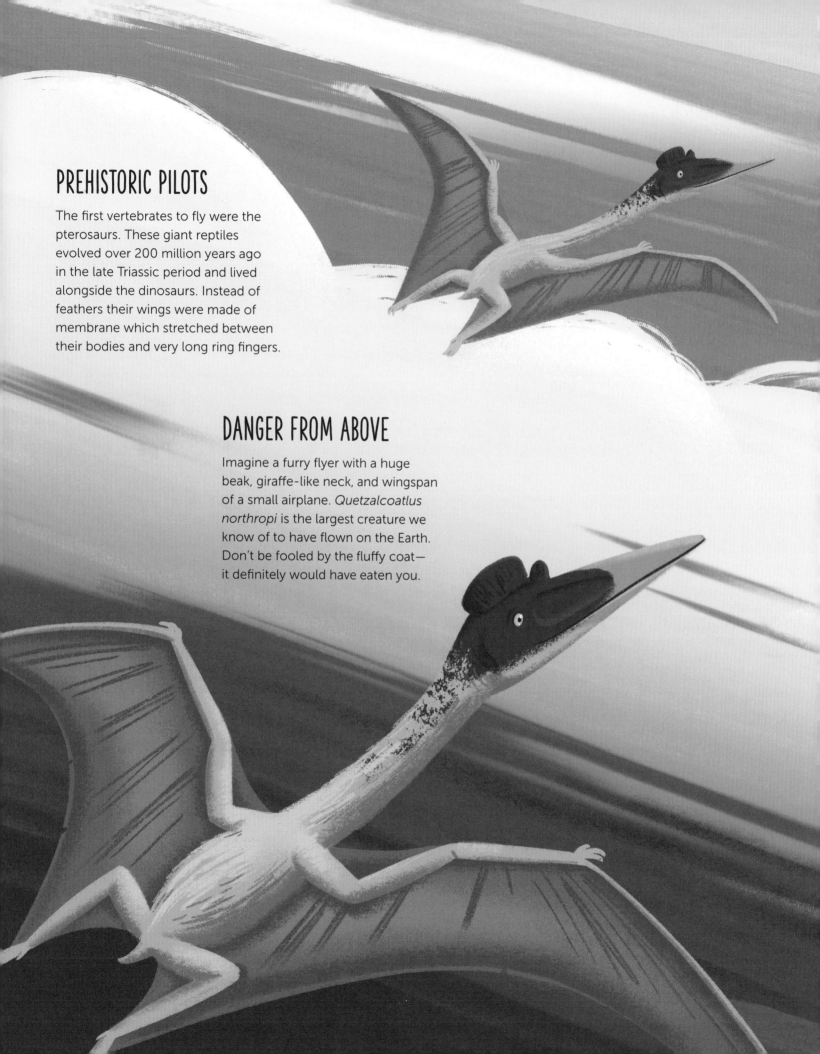

PREHISTORIC PILOTS

The first vertebrates to fly were the pterosaurs. These giant reptiles evolved over 200 million years ago in the late Triassic period and lived alongside the dinosaurs. Instead of feathers their wings were made of membrane which stretched between their bodies and very long ring fingers.

DANGER FROM ABOVE

Imagine a furry flyer with a huge beak, giraffe-like neck, and wingspan of a small airplane. *Quetzalcoatlus northropi* is the largest creature we know of to have flown on the Earth. Don't be fooled by the fluffy coat— it definitely would have eaten you.

HIGH FLIERS

Why walk when you can fly? Living creatures have been taking to the skies in one form or another for the last 400 million years. It's a handy way to move long distances or keep a look out for lunch far below, but it's hard work and those who have mastered it have been practicing a long time.

DO YOU EVEN LIFT?

When you're really big, the hardest part of flying might be getting off the ground in the first place. Pterosaurs, like bats, walked on their folded wings so palaeontologists think they might have used all four limbs to leap into the air and take flight.

AVIAN ANCESTORS

It's true, there really are dinosaurs in your front garden. The birds we see today evolved from theropods, the same family of dinosaurs *Tyrannosaurus rex* came from. No wonder they've got so much to sing about.

WINGIN' IT

Flying is tricky, so it's important to have the right wings for the job. If you live in a forest and need to dart between the trees you'll want short, rounded wings—perfect for fast turns. If you've got a big journey ahead you'll need long, thin wings to glide on the sea breeze. And if you're more of a hoverer you won't need long wings at all—but be ready to flap them as fast as you can.

READY FOR TAKE OFF

Smaller birds like robins and sparrows have elliptical wings, allowing them to take off quickly when they need to escape a predator. They can't maintain this speed for very long but they can perform some pretty impressive aerial acrobatics.

NEED FOR SPEED

Long, pointy wings are designed for speed. Swallows and swifts use their wings to migrate vast distances, while peregrine falcons dive toward their prey at blistering speed. Handy for the falcon, not so lucky for the mouse below.

Eurasian magpie

Northern cardinal

Blue rock-thrush

Goldfinch

Peregrine falcon

Mallard

Hummingbirds

Pacific swift

Barn swallow

HOVER RIGHT THERE

Hummingbirds are so small and light they can hover just by beating their tiny wings fast enough. It takes a huge amount of energy but it means they can go up, down, sideways, and even backwards to poke around for delicious bugs and nectar.

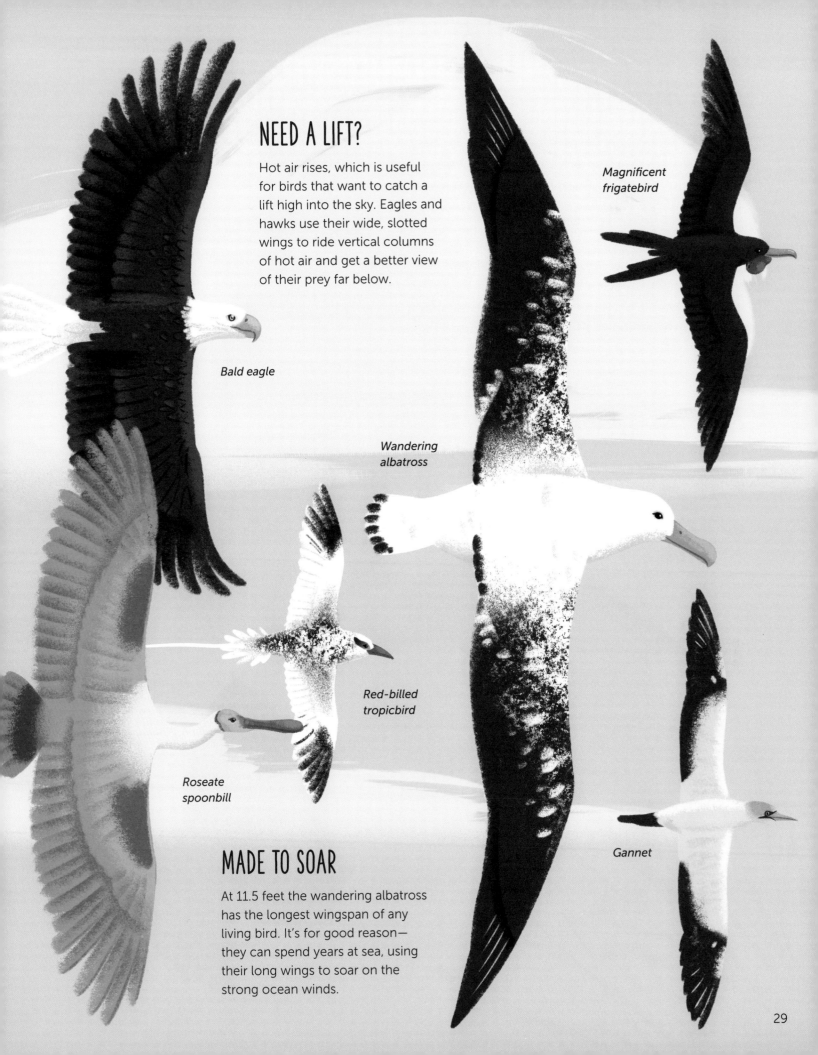

NEED A LIFT?

Hot air rises, which is useful for birds that want to catch a lift high into the sky. Eagles and hawks use their wide, slotted wings to ride vertical columns of hot air and get a better view of their prey far below.

Bald eagle

Magnificent frigatebird

Wandering albatross

Red-billed tropicbird

Roseate spoonbill

Gannet

MADE TO SOAR

At 11.5 feet the wandering albatross has the longest wingspan of any living bird. It's for good reason— they can spend years at sea, using their long wings to soar on the strong ocean winds.

TINY DANCERS

The first animals to fly weren't prehistoric reptiles or feathered birds—they were insects. Fossil evidence shows us that dragonfly-like invertebrates took to the skies some 400 million years ago—long before those with a backbone ever tried.

Some were tiny while others had a wingspan wider than your outstretched arm. Learning how to fly allowed insects to escape predators, cross continents, and evolve into the millions of species we know of today.

FLIGHT CLUB

Insects were the first members of an exclusive animal club—those who achieved flight using their own wing power. Only pterosaurs, birds, and bats have joined since. There are plenty of gliders but they need a bit more help from the wind.

Painted lady butterfly

Emperor dragonfly

Damselfly

Comet moth

Peacock butterfly

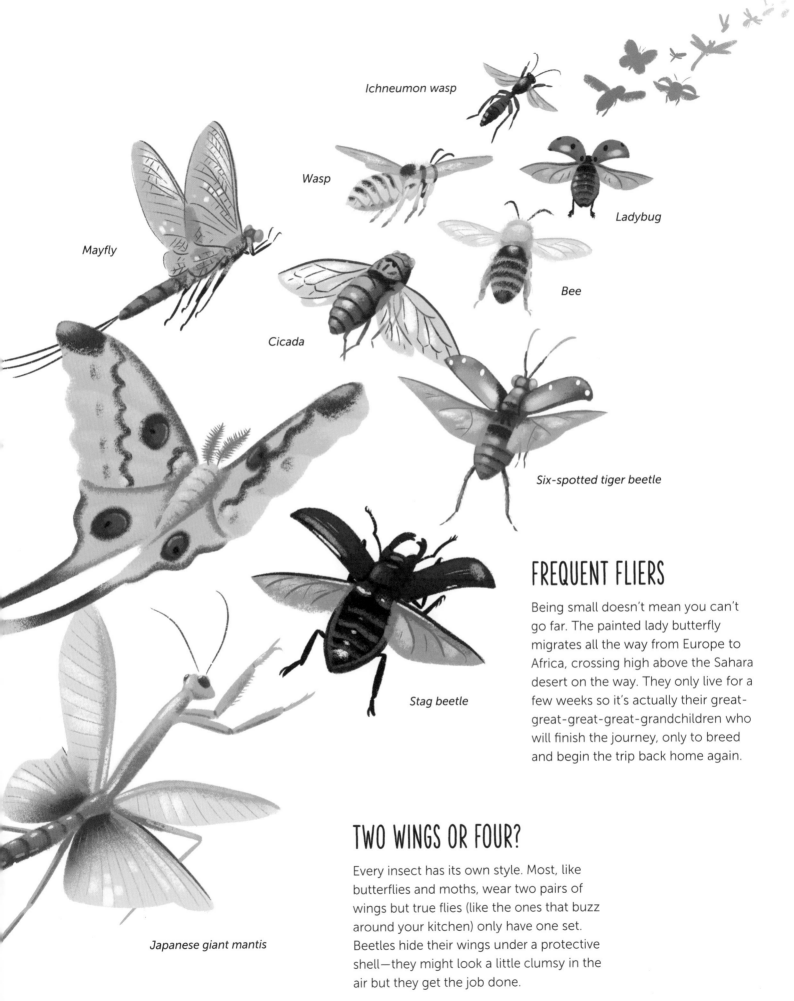

Ichneumon wasp

Wasp

Ladybug

Mayfly

Bee

Cicada

Six-spotted tiger beetle

Stag beetle

Japanese giant mantis

FREQUENT FLIERS

Being small doesn't mean you can't go far. The painted lady butterfly migrates all the way from Europe to Africa, crossing high above the Sahara desert on the way. They only live for a few weeks so it's actually their great-great-great-great-grandchildren who will finish the journey, only to breed and begin the trip back home again.

TWO WINGS OR FOUR?

Every insect has its own style. Most, like butterflies and moths, wear two pairs of wings but true flies (like the ones that buzz around your kitchen) only have one set. Beetles hide their wings under a protective shell—they might look a little clumsy in the air but they get the job done.

FLIGHT PATTERNS

If you're standing in just the right spot as the sun dips below the horizon you might see a dark cloud twisting and turning across the sky. It isn't made of gas or vapour, these are birds—winter starlings settling in to roost.

This formation is called a murmuration, a name that comes from the murmuring sound made by thousands of tiny wings fluttering all at once.

FLOCK-MATES

The starlings in murmurations don't follow a leader, so how do they know where they're going? It would be impossible for each bird to see the whole flock, so scientists think they only need to keep an eye on seven of their neighbours to know the next move.

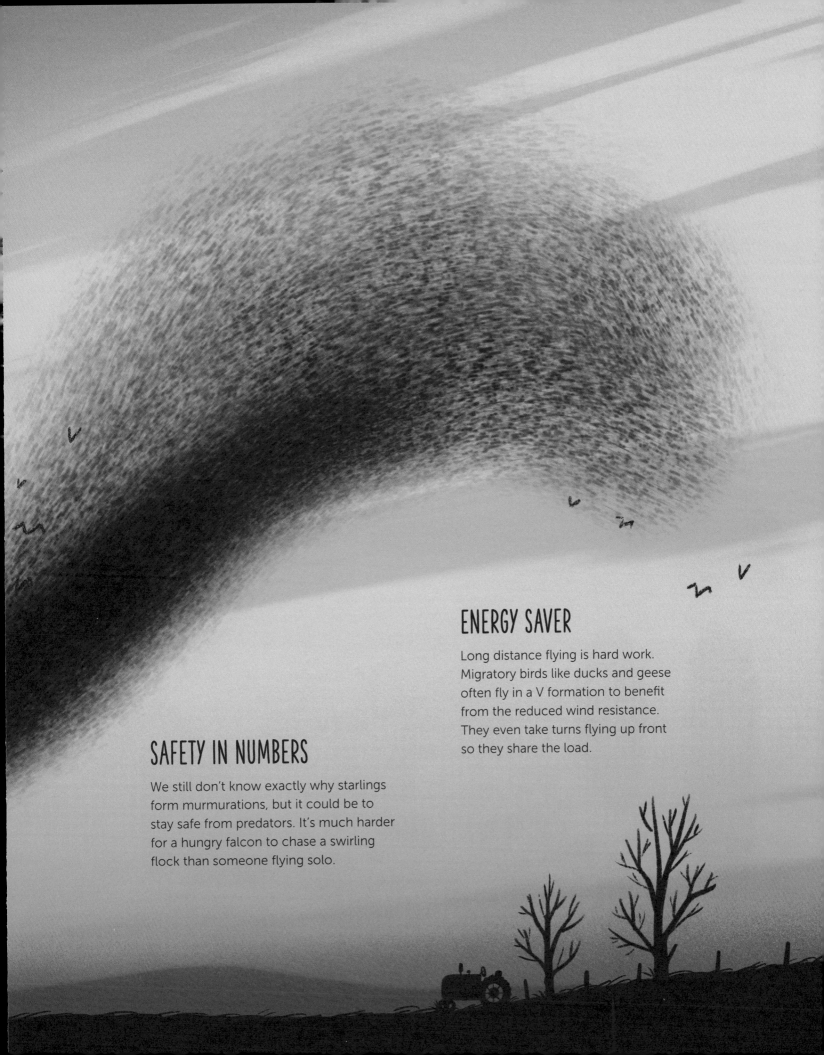

SAFETY IN NUMBERS

We still don't know exactly why starlings
form murmurations, but it could be to
stay safe from predators. It's much harder
for a hungry falcon to chase a swirling
flock than someone flying solo.

ENERGY SAVER

Long distance flying is hard work.
Migratory birds like ducks and geese
often fly in a V formation to benefit
from the reduced wind resistance.
They even take turns flying up front
so they share the load.

INSPIRED BY NATURE

Inventors have always borrowed ideas from the natural world, and none more so than Leonardo Da Vinci. He studied birds and bats in great detail to understand how they fly, with the hope of designing a machine that would launch people to the skies. While he didn't live to see people take flight, his designs inspired countless others to look to nature and build the type of aircraft that we use today.

IF YOU CAN'T BEAT THEM

Da Vinci drew plans for an ornithopter (meaning "bird wing"). Made from silk and wood, its flapping mechanical wings were to be powered by the pilot. It's a great idea on paper but unfortunately humans just don't have the arm strength to stay airborne on their own.

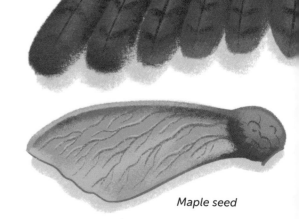

Red kite

Bird skull

LIGHT AS A FEATHER

Birds have evolved to be excellent fliers. Heavy jaw and teeth? Swap it for a beak. Need smooth, light insulation? Try a suit of feathers. Many birds even have hollow bones to store extra oxygen for when they need it most.

Feathers

Maple seed

THE SEED OF AN IDEA

Da Vinci was a bit of an overachiever. As well as his ornithopter, he drew plans for a pyramid-shaped parachute, an early submarine, and even a screw-like helicopter inspired by falling maple seeds.

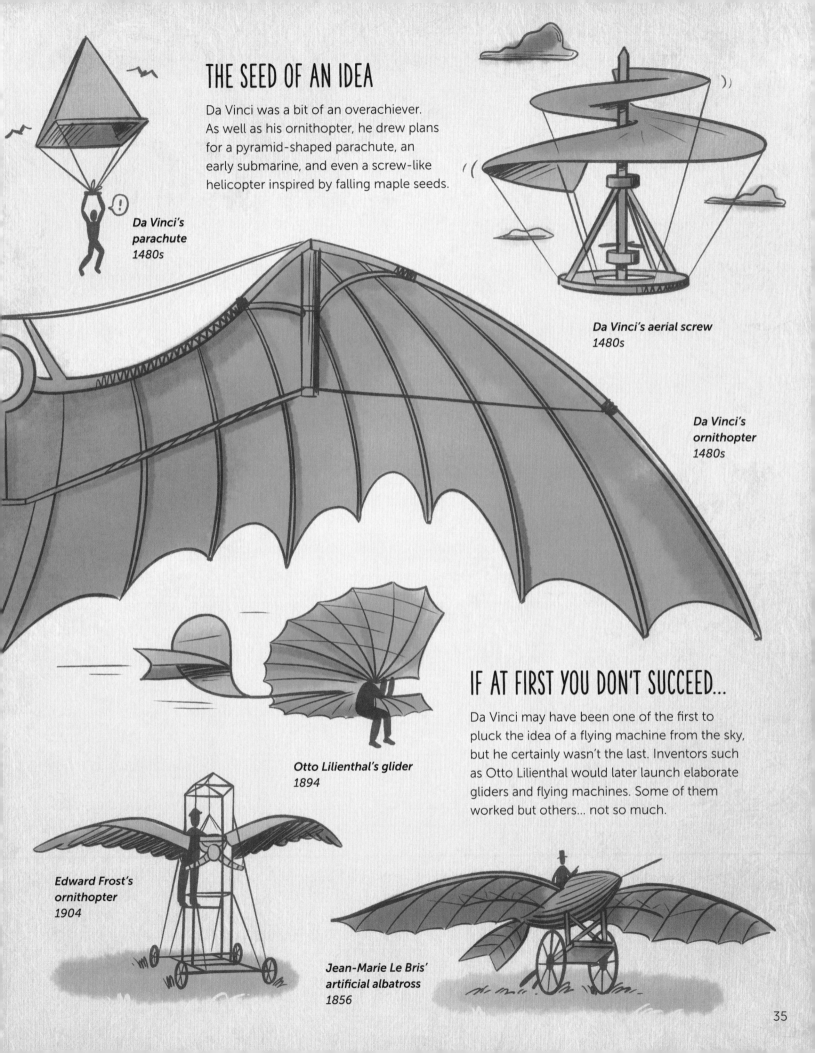

Da Vinci's parachute
1480s

Da Vinci's aerial screw
1480s

Da Vinci's ornithopter
1480s

Otto Lilienthal's glider
1894

IF AT FIRST YOU DON'T SUCCEED...

Da Vinci may have been one of the first to pluck the idea of a flying machine from the sky, but he certainly wasn't the last. Inventors such as Otto Lilienthal would later launch elaborate gliders and flying machines. Some of them worked but others... not so much.

Edward Frost's ornithopter
1904

Jean-Marie Le Bris' artificial albatross
1856

HUMANS IN FLIGHT

Jump up high on a trampoline and you might feel like you're flying—until you come back down again. A few seconds wasn't enough for early aviators, they wanted to stay in the air for as long as they possibly could. There were records to set, wars to win, and later passengers to take. Now we need to fly in a new direction, and it might be the most exciting one yet.

*Montgolfier
hot-air balloon
1783*

*Giffard airship
1852*

EARLY AVIATORS

Imagine being in one of the first flying machines—not made out of wood or aluminium, but paper. The Montgolfier brothers launched their aerostat (hot air balloon) in 1783. However, being lighter than air is one thing, to get something heavier off the ground would require wings.

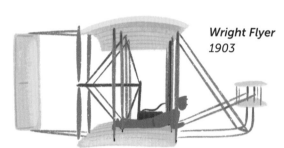

*Wright Flyer
1903*

*Blériot XI
1909*

*Blackburn Type D
1912*

*Deperdussin Type A
1910*

*Antoinette VII
1909*

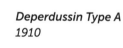

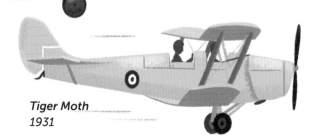

*Royal Aircraft
Factory S.E.5
1916*

*Tiger Moth
1931*

FLYING THROUGH THE DARK

Conflict has had a huge impact on aviation. Planes were first used in war for surveillance but were soon adapted to fight in combat. Many of these pilots lost their lives or caused others to lose theirs, a reminder of the power held by those behind the machines.

TRIUMPH AND TRAGEDY

The 1920s and 1930s saw amazing aviators like Bessie Coleman perform stunts to cheering crowds below, while Amelia Earhart zigzagged across the globe. It was a time of great success, but not one without tragedy—sadly both pilots died in plane accidents.

Lockheed 10E Electra
1934

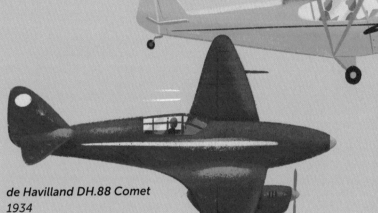

Piper PA-18
Super Cub
1949

Curtiss JN Jenny
1916

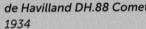

de Havilland DH.88 Comet
1934

Douglas DC-3
1936

Concorde
1976

NOW BOARDING...

Early passenger flights were expensive and uncomfortable, but as the planes got bigger and flew higher it became quite the glamorous pastime. As more airlines appeared, everyday people had a chance to fly, changing the way we travel forever.

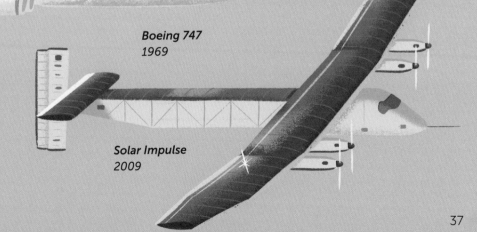

Boeing 747
1969

THE FUTURE OF FLIGHT

We can't keep flying the way we do now. Jet fuel releases carbon dioxide into the atmosphere, contributing to climate change. Luckily we're working on an alternative. Aircraft like the *Solar Impulse 2* have already circumnavigated the globe using only the power of the sun.

Solar Impulse
2009

THE ROOF OF THE WORLD

Almost all of the world's tallest mountains can be found in the Himalayas. Everest stands at 29,029 feet, with her neighbors Kangchenjunga, Lhotse, and Makalu not that far below.

EYES ON THE TOP

Tenzing Norgay and Edmund Hillary were the first to climb to the top of Everest in 1953. Since then thousands of others have stood on its summit, but tragically many others have lost their lives trying.

SACRED SUMMITS

Mountains are sacred places. Sagarmatha, Chomolungma, and Mount Everest are all names for the same peak but for some people she's a mother goddess to be respected and for others a trophy to conquer.

HIGH PEAKS

Unwrap a sheet of crumpled paper and you can hold the Himalayas in your hand. Deep ravines rise to sharp peaks, and in the middle stands the highest of them all—Everest. This incredible mountain range was formed millions of years ago when two continents collided, and they've slowly been moving closer ever since.

MOUNTAIN LIFE

Survival high in the mountains is tough, but that's not to say that nothing lives up here. Himalayan tahrs and musk deer graze on the forested foothills while snow leopards prowl the rocky cliffs above. Even tiny spiders have been spotted high on the mountain side.

STILL GROWING

Mountains can't grow, right? The tectonic plates that collided to form the Himalayas are still moving, so Mount Everest is slowly getting taller. It's only by about 5mm a year so it will take a long time before anyone

THE RIGHT ALTITUDE

The Himalayas are home to a diverse range of creatures. From the grassy plains to the jagged cliffs, every animal that lives here has adapted to survive in extreme conditions. Many are shy and prefer to blend into the landscape. Others are loud and proud— bright streaks of gold and blue against the snowy skyline.

Red panda

HOLD MY COAT

For high-altitude mammals, a good coat is a must. Himalayan marmots have dense, woolly fur—perfect for staying cosy during a long winter hibernation. Red pandas wear two layers—a thick, soft undercoat and bushy hair on top. They can even wrap themselves in their own tail for a little extra warmth.

Himalayan marmot

Himalayan pit viper

Snow leopard

SPOT THE DIFFERENCE

If you're looking for a snow leopard, chances are they're already watching you – hidden in the rocky mountains above. Known as "ghost cats," these solitary hunters are experts at remaining unseen. But even ghosts like the snow leopard are threatened by habitat loss and poaching.

THE HIGHEST BEAKS

There's a party in the sky over the Himalayas. Alpine choughs twist and twirl high above while a pair of black-necked cranes dance to impress on the plateau below. But when it comes to fancy dress, no one beats the vibrant plumage of the Himalayan monal.

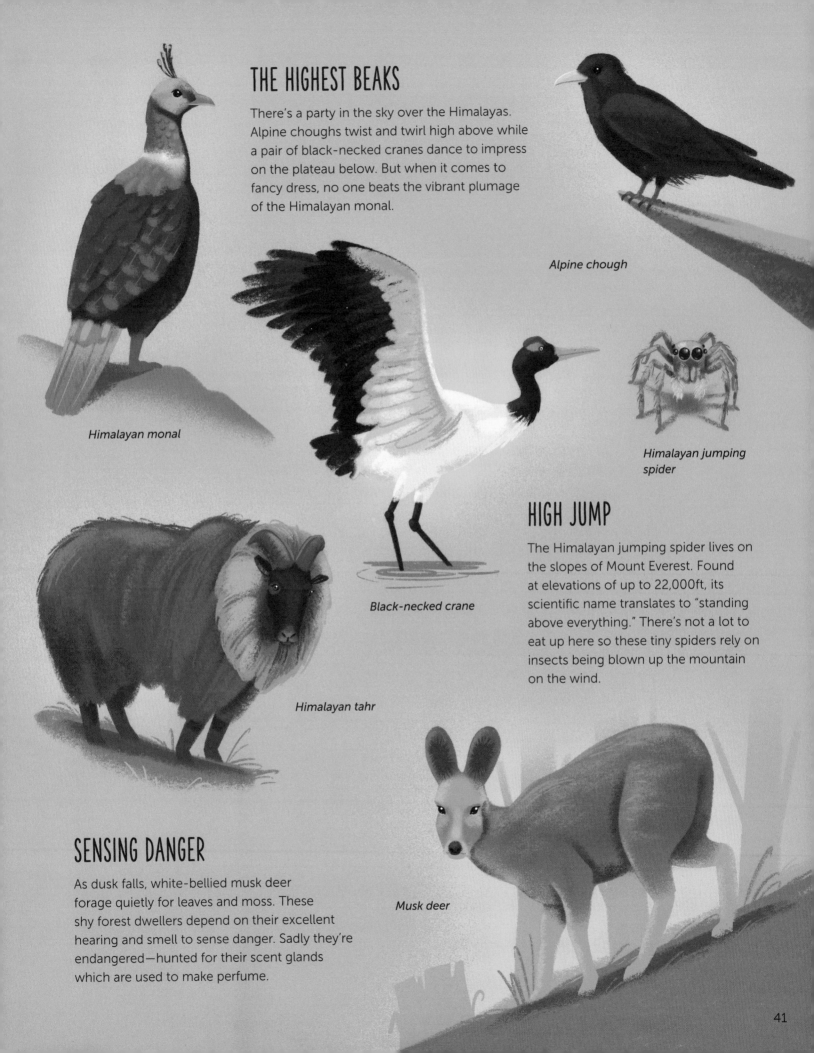

Alpine chough

Himalayan monal

Himalayan jumping spider

Black-necked crane

HIGH JUMP

The Himalayan jumping spider lives on the slopes of Mount Everest. Found at elevations of up to 22,000ft, its scientific name translates to "standing above everything." There's not a lot to eat up here so these tiny spiders rely on insects being blown up the mountain on the wind.

Himalayan tahr

SENSING DANGER

As dusk falls, white-bellied musk deer forage quietly for leaves and moss. These shy forest dwellers depend on their excellent hearing and smell to sense danger. Sadly they're endangered—hunted for their scent glands which are used to make perfume.

Musk deer

HOME IN THE MOUNTAINS

Namaste! You've climbed up high into the Himalayas. Even though we're thousands of feet above sea level, you're still in the shadow of the world's tallest peaks. Winding roads and suspended bridges connect terraced villages that cling to the side of the mountain. A car won't be much use up here. Instead, try a good pair of walking shoes and a yak.

YAK POWER

If you hear the soft clanging of bells up here it might be a herd of Yaks coming through. These hairy helpers have been used to carry heavy loads across the Himalayas for centuries. Their milk is used for food, their wool for knitting, and their poop as fuel.

CLIMBING CULTURES

Sherpas are an ethnic group of people from high in the mountains of Nepal. Traditionally farmers, some Sherpas became excellent mountaineers when tourists realized they couldn't get to the top without their expert help. Climbing can make a lot more money than growing potatoes, but it has its own cost too.

CHANGING MOUNTAINS

Mountain life is changing. While nomadic yak shepherds used to be commonplace in the Himalayas, younger generations are now choosing different paths or moving to big cities instead. But you always carry your home with you, no matter how far away you are.

DANGEROUS DREAMS

If you've ever climbed up a tree you might know what it feels like to be on top of the world. Some people don't stop at trees, they move on to mountains and only the tallest will do. Mountaineers are determined people, but things can go wrong up high and it's important to remember when to come back down.

SUMMIT FEVER

Getting stuck in a line at the supermarket is annoying, but a queue up here can be deadly. Everest can only be attempted for a few weeks of the year when the weather is just right which can lead to a long, cold wait for the top.

A TAN ON EVEREST?

Mountaineers need to be prepared for not just the extreme cold but also the intense solar glare that reflects off the ice. Eye protection is a must—beach umbrella not required.

Climbing goggles

Rope

Carabiner

Ice axe

Ice screw

Old-fashioned oxygen kit

THINNING AIR

The higher you go, the thinner the air gets. Most climbers use bottled oxygen to help them reach the summit of Everest, but that means they need to carry it all the way up and leave enough to get back down again.

A MOUNTAIN OF TRASH

The slopes of Mount Everest are littered with plastic, old rope, and empty oxygen tanks. Thankfully new laws mean the mountain is slowly being cleared of trash.

Trash

EXOSPHERE

Up to 6,200 miles high

The last layer of our atmosphere is a bit of a blur. The air in the exosphere is extremely thin and gradually fades into the vastness of space. Bye Earth.

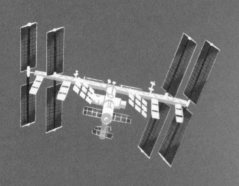

THERMOSPHERE

Up to 370 miles high

The thermosphere absorbs most of the X-ray and UV radiation from the Sun, so it's no wonder things start to heat up here. It's a crowded place where satellites and telescopes orbit the Earth, and it's only getting busier.

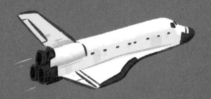

Kármán line

MESOSPHERE

Up to 50 miles high

If you think about the atmosphere like an ocean, the mesosphere is where things start to get choppy. Strong winds and gravity waves surge around this freezing cold layer, and it's also where most meteors burn up on their way to Earth.

Ozone layer

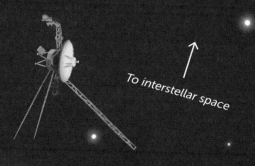

To interstellar space

HIGH SKIES

Space is cold, so the Earth needs to wear a few sweaters—five to be exact. But unlike the knitted one you got for your last birthday, these atmospheric layers can absorb radiation, burn up meteors, and keep our precious air from being sucked into space. It's probably best to hand wash.

TROPOSPHERE

Up to 9 miles high

If you get caught in the rain you can blame the troposphere. This dense, wet layer is full of air and water vapour on the move, forming our clouds and weather systems. It's thickest around the equator and thinnest at the poles.

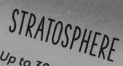

STRATOSPHERE

Up to 30 miles high

In the stratosphere, the higher you go the warmer it gets. It's where you'll find the ozone layer, a sunscreen-like shield that absorbs solar radiation. Commercial aircraft and some birds poke their beaks up here to take advantage of the smooth ride.

CLOUD SPOTTING

If you spend a lot of time with your head in the clouds you might decide to become a meteorologist (someone who studies weather). These scientists keep watch for wispy cirrus clouds, cauliflower-like cumulus, or an ominous-looking nimbus.

Nimbostratus

Cirrostratus

KNOW YOUR NIMBUS

Clouds are named for their size, shape and where they sit in the atmosphere. Stratus clouds hang low, alto clouds are mid-level and cirrus clouds float high above. Nimbus clouds are full of water vapor and are likely to ruin a picnic.

Altocumulus

Altostratus

Cumulus

PROUD OF YOUR CLOUDS

Clouds aren't just an Earth thing. Venus makes mustard-yellow clouds of sulfuric acid, Jupiter has a storm of swirling ammonia brewing, and Mars wears rainbow clouds made from shards of shimmering ice.

Cumulonimbus

Cirrus

Cirrocumulus

KEEP IT COOL

When you think about extinction, clouds might
not come to mind. As our planet warms and
the chemical mix in our atmosphere changes,
certain types of clouds might start to disappear.
It could be a big problem, because clouds
like stratocumulus actually cool our home by
reflecting the Sun's rays.

Stratocumulus

Stratus

HIGH STAKES

The atmosphere high above your head is a soupy mix of nitrogen, oxygen, and a sprinkle of other gases. It's the perfect recipe for life to thrive on our tiny planet.

Except the mix is changing, fast. The fossil fuels we burn have made the air thick with carbon dioxide and other gases—trapping heat and warming our home. We've got a window of time to avert the worst impacts, but it's closing fast.

TALK ABOUT A REVOLUTION

If you needed a new chair in the 1700s, you'd visit someone who made chairs. Beautiful, handmade chairs. Then we had a clever idea—what if you had a factory to make lots of chairs really quickly? You could make steam engines, riveted planes, and steel motorcars in factories too. This was the beginning of the Industrial Revolution and our reliance on fossil fuels.

FUEL FOR THOUGHT

300 million years ago, the Earth was a swampy, squelchy place. Plants that died decomposed, slowly turning into peat and then fossil fuels like coal, oil, and natural gas. All of that energy wasn't lost, it was stored deep underground until people realized it could be dug up and burned for power.

BLUE SKIES AHEAD

This is scary stuff, but it's important to remember that every time humans have faced huge challenges we've worked together to overcome them. We have the technology we need to power our world from the wind and the sun, and the compassion to make sure it's fair for everyone who lives here.

RISING RISKS

Draw a line of our rising CO_2 emissions and it would be steeper than the mountains in this book. As the global population has increased, so too has our dependence on fossil fuels—something we drastically need to cut to limit the impacts of climate change. Luckily unlike climbing a mountain, it's up to us when we reach the peak and start heading back down.

THE VIEW FROM UP HERE

If you were to catch a lift into space (and maybe one day you will) you could look back down at Earth. You'd see vast oceans, swirling clouds, and snow-capped mountains. Then, as night creeps across the globe, you could watch our cities light up and count just how many of us there are.

All of this is wrapped in the thin blanket of our atmosphere. We've already managed to poke holes in it, and if we keep living the way we do it could be lost forever. We can't buy another one, but if we look after it we might not need to.

THE WORLD TREE

In Norse mythology, the vast tree Yggdrasil grows in the center of the universe. Its roots and branches link the nine worlds, including Ásgard (the realm of the gods) and Midgard (the human realm).

VOYAGE TO VALHALLA

The Vikings believed that brave warriors killed in combat would journey to Valhalla, a great hall in the heavens. It was ruled by the god Odin, and there they would feast until they fought at Ragnarök, the end of days.

The northern lights (or *aurora borealis*) have shimmered their way into the stories of many cultures. Some saw dancing souls, others a warning of hardships to come. In Finland the lights were thought to be sparks lit by the tail of a mythical firefox as it ran through the forest.

HIGH HEAVENS

Look up at the night sky and you'll share a view with people that lived thousands of years before. They watched the same dazzling stars and fiery comets as we do today. But while we're able to understand them with science, ancient cultures explained them with myths—stories of gods and titans fighting great battles across the cosmos.

SKY GODS

Being a human in ancient times could be tough. Drought, plagues, forgetting to buy milk. It made sense to see every problem as the work of a god, and every culture had their own.

HIGH AND MIGHTY

The Sun is the bringer of life, and so too were many of the ancient gods and goddesses connected to it. The Egyptian god Ra rode his golden barque (a type of ship) across the heavens to give the world light.

Amaterasu
Shintō Sun goddess

Arinnitti
Hittite Sun goddess

Ra
*Egyptian
Sun god*

Apollo
Greek Sun god

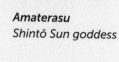

A DEITY IN THE LIFE

Ancient gods are still part of our everyday lives. In English, most of our weekdays are named after Norse gods like Thor (Thursday). The planets with which we share our solar system take their names from Greek and Roman gods too.

STAR GODS

The Moon is often associated with change and new life. It waxes, wanes, or disappears completely – only to be reborn all over again.

IT'S A TWIN THING

Many celestial gods are twins. The Ancient Egyptians worshipped Geb as the god of the earth and his sister Nut as goddess of the sky. In Greek mythology Artemis is linked with the Moon while her twin brother Apollo is the god of the Sun.

Artemis
Greek Moon goddess

Coyolxauhqui
Aztec Moon goddess

Nannar
Mesopotamian Moon god

Nótt
Norse giantess

YOUR CHARIOT AWAITS

If you're going to cross the vast heavens you'll need transportation. The Hindu god Chandra drives an antelope-drawn chariot while the Norse giantess Nótt rides her horse Hrimfaxi (frost mane) across the inky-black night.

Chandra
Hindu Moon god

STORIES IN THE STARS

The world above your head is a crowded place. A giant bear roars to her cub, an eagle soars through the milky way, and winged Pegasus canters across the cosmos. Humans have found shapes in the stars for as long as they've looked up, and you can too.

Aquila

Ursa Major

NAVIGATING THE STARS

If you know a star will be in a certain spot in the sky you can use it to find your way home. Sailors have used constellations to navigate for centuries, just as they do today.

Pegasus

SAME STARS, DIFFERENT SHAPES

People see different things in the night sky. The stars of Scorpius look like a scorpion to some and a snake to others. Distant cultures came up with remarkably similar ideas though—Orion is often seen as a warrior, even by people on opposite sides of the Earth.

Scorpius

Emu in the Sky

DARK CONSTELLATIONS

While western cultures look for shapes in the stars, many Aboriginal Australians and Torres Strait Islanders see constellations in the space between them. The Emu in the Sky is stretched out across the dark clouds of the Milky Way.

Azure Dragon

Lepus

SKY DRAGONS

Four mythical creatures stood guard over the skies of Ancient China. The Azure Dragon to the East, the Black Tortoise to the North, the White Tiger to the West, and the Red Bird to the South. Each represents a different season and is made up of many smaller constellations.

Orion

SKY LINES

The sky's a busy place. Human and animal aviators zigzag across the globe to break records, migrate across oceans, and to watch our world from above.

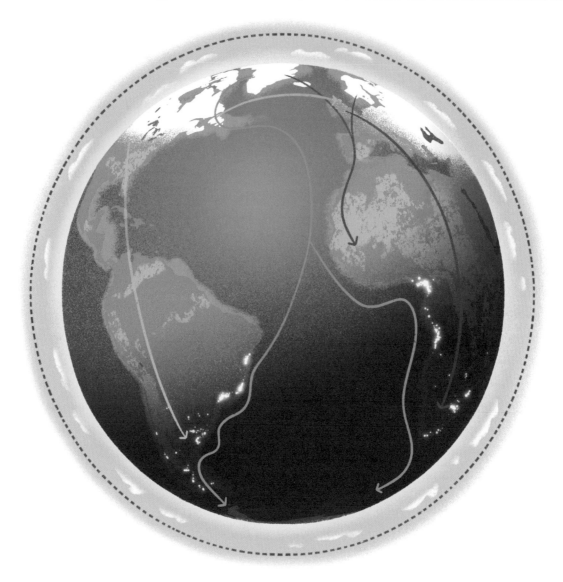

 **Amelia Earhart's 1932 flight**
2,026 miles solo record

 Painted lady migration
8,700 miles round trip

 **International Space Station**
Orbits Earth every 90 minutes

 Arctic tern migration
18,600 miles round trip

 Barn swallow migration
12,400 miles round trip

 Swainson's hawk migration
12,000 miles round trip

RULES OF FLIGHT

Those who have mastered the art of flying have been practicing for a long time. Take a feather out of their wing and see what it takes to soar among the clouds.

WHAT GOES UP...

If you're lighter than air, you'll rise. Most of us aren't, which is where gases like hot air, hydrogen and helium come in handy. Don't forget to cool your jets and come back down to Earth or else you might end up in the stratosphere.

PUT A WING ON IT

If there's a must-have accessory for flying it's your wings. These fancy flappers come in canvas, feathers, or even your own skin. Long and pointy are for speed, short and curvy for style.
Why stop at just one? Try a pair, four, or even more.

SIZE MATTERS

Being small is a big advantage when it comes to flight. That pesky gravity can't keep you down, and if you beat your wings fast enough you might start to hover. It's why trillions of tiny insects take to the sky and why elephants generally don't.

THRUST IS A MUST

It's all well and good to float upwards, but if you want to go forward you'll need thrust. Rev your engines, beat your wings, and take a running leap into the air. You can tilt your wings if you want to slow down but it's a bit of a drag.

FIND YOUR FLOCK

The only thing better than flying is doing it with friends. Grab your gaggle and start practicing your flight formation. There's safety in numbers, and if you get the timing just right you can make beautiful patterns across the sky.

BE NICE TO THE BIRDS

They come from a family of dinosaurs after all.

GLOSSARY

Arboreal creatures that live in the branches of trees.

Avian describes something that is related to birds.

Aviation the flying or operating of an aircraft.

Carbon a chemical element that is safely stored in plants, soil, and trees. The destruction of these things releases their carbon into the atmosphere and contributes to climate change.

Chlorophyll a green pigment, commonly found in plants and trees, that is responsible for the absorption of light to provide energy for growing. This process is called photosynthesis.

Depth perception the ability to see things in three dimensions (length, width, and depth) and to accurately judge how far away an object is.

Fungal network underground networks created by fungi that connect plants with each other and can transfer water, carbon, nitrogen, and other nutrients and minerals.

Industrial Revolution a time when the manufacturing of goods moved from small shops and homes to large factories. This shift brought about changes in culture as people moved from rural areas to big cities in order to work.

Invertebrate a creature without a backbone, such as an insect, spider, or earthworm.

Monoliths a large single upright block, usually made of stone, that serves as a pillar, marker or monument.

Prehensile usually refers to an animal's limb or tail that is capable of grasping tree branches.

Rewilding to restore an area of land to its natural state. It is also used to describe the action of reintroducing species of animals to areas where they once thrived but were driven out or exterminated.

Solar radiation a general term for the radiation emitted by the Sun. On Earth it is scattered and filtered through the atmosphere. It can be captured and turned into useful forms of energy, such as electricity.

Taiga a type of wet and swampy pine and spruce forest, found in the far northern parts of the world. It is sometimes called a snow forest.

Vertebrate a creature with a backbone, such as a mammal or a reptile.

Wind resistance the force an object must overcome to move through the air.

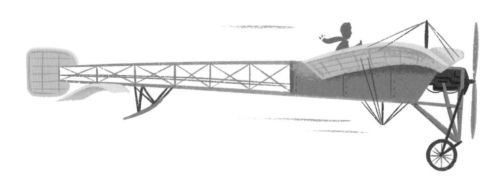

INDEX